Abdulrahman Al-Banna was born in Dubai in 1996 and was raised in a family-oriented household. He fell in love with writing ever since he was a little boy and started creating his own characters and stories. He now holds a Bachelor's degree in petroleum engineering and a Master's program in skills of a TV director. He is dedicated to supporting those he loves and helping those in need.

Writing became his El Dorado when it comes to expressing his more personal thoughts and setting his emotions free.

To those who are battling demons every day, may you find the strength you need on your journey to self-discovery.

Abdulrahman AlBanna

UNTITLED FOR NOW

AUSTIN MACAULEY PUBLISHERS™

LONDON • CAMBRIDGE • NEW YORK • SHARJAH

ISBN – 9789948770183 – (Paperback)
ISBN – 9789948770190 – (E-Book)

Application Number: MC-10-01-7452524
Age Classification: E

Printer Name: iPrint Global Ltd
Printer Address: Witchford, England

First Published 2024
AUSTIN MACAULEY PUBLISHERS FZE
Sharjah Publishing City
P.O Box [519201]
Sharjah, UAE
www.austinmacauley.ae
+971 655 95 202

First of all, I would like to thank my family for their constant love and support.

I would also like to extend my gratitude to my dearest friends – without you guys this book would still be a dream.

Special thanks to Rawan and Meri for helping me bring this book to life.

Abadii for being the beacon of light when I was in darkness.

GMASBR, BC, WHCE, love you all.

Allure of Darkness

The allure of darkness is very strong, temptation
It pulls you toward a never-ending leave
Burns out your lungs, suffocation
Drowning, unable to breathe
No process, devastation
Alone in a dream
No chances, recreation
Being your own fear.

Alone

Alone
No protection
On my own
No redemption
No change
Nothing strange
Just a view
And an assumption
Growing older
Growing wise
Being bolder
Able to rise
Alone
Standing
Nowhere to go
Alone
Stranded
No one to know.

I Had a Dream

And then you'd start a conversation saying,
"I had a dream."
I had a dream and you were there
There was a demon, you were scared
We were both flying in the air
I had a dream…

Love Eclipse

I was the sun
You were the moon
We had our fun
Now it's ending too soon
I call my mum
You call your friends
I tell her it's done
You tell them 'tis the end

When we first met
I thought you were cute
It was in my head
When I couldn't refute
All the things that you said
Even though you were wrong
So I loved you instead
Now I'm singing this song

And when I sing
You do not know
That if you listen
You can hear my woe

And when we say goodbye
To the ones we once loved
We never feel the same way
'Cause we know they changed us
Dearly beloved,
I will never forget you
You will always be in my heart
'Cause we are used to being apart.

My Therapy

I didn't know I would cave in
Spend 20 days craving
The way you put your arms around me

After a while, I just gave in
Gave you all the love I was saving
Hoping it would make you stay with me

You give me 30 reasons to smile
And 50 reasons to try
All the reasons to be happy

And you wipe my tears when I cry
Call me out when I lie
You've become my therapy

And I'm falling head-over-heel
All those feelings that I feel
Were never meant to be for you

But my heart, you did steal
All of this is now real
And the love that I feel is true

God, I hope
You and me
Are meant to be
Because you
Make me
So happy
Just like therapy.

Silver Hair and Eyes of Blue

I tell myself every time I see your eyes
That true love exists
In the midst of all our lies
I try to think rationally
But I can't
Because
It's you who I want.

Dearly Beloved

I felt your presence again today
You were there… sitting in the crowded auditorium as they
called out my name
I was able to feel how proud you were of me
I imagined that smile on your face… the warmth it gave me
I heard your voice among all the voices congratulating me
A faint whisper… "You did good."
I smiled.
Everyone wanted to celebrate
I told them to go ahead
And I came here instead…
I miss you, you know?
I miss all the kind words you ever said to me
I miss your warm hug… your smile… your voice
But I felt your presence
I know you can hear this
And I know you can't come back
I want you to know…
One memory lingers in my head
That day I made you upset
I think I was too loud
I was being insensible

I annoyed you
I'm sorry
You were already in pain
I swear I will not do it again
I'm sorry
Please forgive me…

I looked up to you… I still do
And I will always be grateful to have known you
I hope you finally found peace
But please
Forgive me
Stay by my side
I still need you
Dearly beloved.

Last Fallen Angel

You brought me down on my knees
Had me begging for mercy
You're like ice-cold water
And a fatal disease
I was too young and pure
I thought you were my cure
All that time and I never knew
What the devil can really do
Break the soul of the last fallen angel
So much for my perfect ending
No more fun in the time I'm spending
All my feelings decomposed
At the time you were exposed
Then you got me down on my knees
I never could admit defeat
You're a killer virus of a summer breeze.

Journey

I'm on my way, I am on my own
I'm almost there, I'll reach my home
A five-year journey on an empty road.

No One

No one wants you
No one likes you
No one thinks you are that smart
No one loves you
No one knows you
No one has you in their heart.

Blank Masterpiece

You keep dwelling over something that was once a masterpiece
But now is just a simple blank page
You thought you got over it
Then you saw the past and started feeling strange
If you ever go back
Will it ever be the same
Keep yourself together, don't play this game
If you ever think that
The fault is yours
Then think again
Keep holding on to strength
You will overcome the pain.

Gone, Gone Away

I knew that something was up
When you were not in your bed
But I thought it was just the demons in my head
And I knew you were gone
When your toothbrush wasn't there
But I thought 'twas my eyesight, for my glasses need repair
I saw your keys were missing
And your hat and cloak
Although 'twas a day off, I said you were off to work
I found your cupboard empty
You even took your best perfume
I lied to myself and said that this wasn't your room
I couldn't find your mug
When I was making tea
I said you took it to Starbucks to fill it with coffee
All your heels were taken
And your car was not in sight
I sat watching the sunset and said you'll be back by night.

Choice

Too lazy to write
Too lazy to think
Too tired to fight
Too tired to sing
I can't even shout loud
Can't hear my own voice
I can't even whisper out,
"This wasn't my choice."

Silver Hair and Eyes of Blue II

I want everything I never had
From the time that I was two
Every toy I never got
Silver hair and eyes of blue
I want everything I broke and lost
All my dreams to turn out true
But I will throw them all out
If I can have you
I want everything that you are
For everything that I am
Everything we ever were
Ever to be a love story
A mystery
It's you who I want.

State Insane

Sometimes all I need is pain
To bring me back from state insane
And one day it will all be fine
But until then I'll stay alive
Try to survive…
Look away 'cause I'm bleeding tears
Can't have you see my inner fears
You're breaking my broken heart
I lost my soul; it broke us apart.

A Boy with a Dream

I am a boy who dreamed to star in a movie of his own
Sing the next top chart number one hit song
Publish a bestseller book
Have people get hooked – on me
They'll be begging for more of me…
While I'm sitting in my room alone
Sipping my wine as I dine alone
Saying I'm fine as I cry alone
Got no-one by my side
But my fame and my broken pride
I'm a boy who used to dream to be a star.

Waiting

I got tired of waiting
For someone that's never coming back
I got bored of sitting in the living room
Way past 3 am on a Wednesday night
Waiting for him to walk through the front door again
And I'm sick of all the memories
That haunt me
In my sleep, when I eat, and in every single shower
I'm fed up of all the times I stared at my phone
Hoping he would call
But I end up alone
Every single time
I cannot take this anymore
I cannot hate this anymore
Can't escape this anymore
Cannot fake it no more
I need to let it go
No!
I need to let me go
To set me free
From thee.

Numb

You're falling down and feeling cold
Losing hope in this human world
Everything feels ever so numb.

Better

I never meant to hurt you
Didn't want to break you
All I wanted was to make us better
Your heart is made of steel I…
never meant to steal it
All I tried was to keep it safer.

One More Time

Take me back to hell on Earth
Take me back to where I was hurt
Show me how to be strong again
And tell me how to fight this pain
Bring me back to when I left
Over the oceans that I have swept
Fly me through a thunderstorm
Then take me back to my old home
Let me go I changed my mind
I cannot face them one more time
I need to take some time away
So, bring me back another day.

Allure of Darkness II

The allure of darkness is very weak, redemption
Pull yourself away
Fill up your lungs, strengthen
No need to stay
No failure, deception
Together we lay
Last chance, confession
The fear never goes away.

Groundless Sky

I go to sleep like a turtle
Wake up and walk in circles
Lost in thoughts again
I wash my face in cold water
Blood running like it's slaughter
But I feel no pain
Lost in dark thoughts is what I fear
I hope for hope but it's not here
I close my eyes then back to sleep
And that is when I start to dream
I dream of wings to let me fly
Escape this world into the sky
Where the rain would fall whenever I cry
To hide my tears in misty clouds
The sky is better than the ground
But since I can't fly I hide in my shell
To escape this unwanted endless hell.

Fractured Mirror

You lost the love you thought was yours forever
Never felt more alone than when we're together
We're a broken piece of heart and a fractured mirror
We're meant to be apart but we're growing nearer.

Brotherhood

35

Brotherhood, such hideous dreams
Meaningless words, and wordless means
Progress not made, progress not seen
One step we take, two back we feel
Pain, regretful tears
Redemption attempts, attempts of fear
In sorrow we met, to darkness we leave
Together we slept, in eternal sleep
Brotherhood, such a shameful word
Step-less stairs in a pitiful world.

Ache

I would do
Whatever it takes
To be with you
And stop your ache

I can't keep living my life like it's all okay
Knowing you will never be mine one day
Should've never let you leave my sight
Should've stood up more
Should've fought another fight
I would fight
Fight
Fight
For you

'Cause leaving you
Was a mistake
I know is huge
But now I'm awake.

Void

You drag me down
Into the void
An endless loop
We can't avoid
You drag me down
To a lonely pit
A desolate town
Filled with misfits
I feel out of place
Out of order
A bit disgraced
I feel a bit left out
A bit outspoken
Out of doubt
You dragged me down
And now I fell
I can't get up
And I couldn't tell
That
You dragged me down

Made me unwell
You were my doom
My endless hell.

Two People

Two people
Is all I need
One for love
One for pain
Both to set me free
’Cause who needs 37 friends
When only two stay till the end.

Love Commits

I know it takes a painful time
To realize that love's a crime
That only daring can commit
Yet none of them to love commits.

Opposites

I'll teach you how to smile if you teach me how to cry
I'll show how to live if you show me how to die
I'll be the positive
I will be your opposite
Be the yin to your yang; show you how to be human
Darkness doesn't need the light
It's the star who needs the night
'Cause it only shines when it's dark
The sunlight comes and there goes the sparks
Teach me how to survive this world
I'll teach how to revive a dead soul
That is gone for too long
I'll teach you to live among the dead
If you show me how to walk ahead
Not fall behind along the road
Here comes the dawn
Leaving up the moon and the stars that shined
Will be gone so soon
I'll let you survive if you let me drive off the road
Onto the path of gold
And be left I'll be right; be darkness I'll be light
I'll bring the day when you bring the night

Forget the peace it's time to fight
Yin yang, left right,
Up down, upside down
Front back, light dark,
You will smile, and I will frown.

42

Silver Hair and Eyes of Blue III

Nothing could ever stand in our way
Not distance, nor time
I want you
So forever be mine
I want everything that you are
For everything that I am
For everything we ever were
Forever to be
A love story and a mystery
For you and me
For it's you who I want
So forever be MINE.

Reason

I see no reason for you to be angry

I see no reason to be mad

I see no reason to be one bit suspicious about everything that makes me glad.

Control

I'm used to being alone here in my zone
I tried to take a peek out; you forced me to stay inside
You're losing hope
That was amidst
All the wrongs
That you did
You lost it all
You feel upset
You're going home
To cry in bed

While my shoulder is empty
And my heart is filled for you
My ears were made to hear your sound
I wish you would tell me your story; whole
You can fly up high 'cause I'll be your ground
I wish you knew that, with me, you'll never lose control.

Death's Tune

Do you know what it means
When your world is falling apart
Do you know how it feels
When you always clutch your heart

When the air all around you
Won't settle in your lungs
When your body starts aching
Even though you're very young
When your vision's all blurry
And the world just spins around
When the people talk around you
But you cannot hear a sound
When you wake up the next morning
As you forgot what you said
When there's nothing but sorrow
And demons in your head
When your stomach is empty
But you cannot take a bite
When the darkness seeps through
And takes away all the light…
You think, *How is it ending so soon,*
Death is now playing its tune.

I Had a Dream II

I had a dream where you'd come and rescue me
Sing a little song that would somehow set me free
I know you'd fight all my demons at the count of three
Play our favorite song as you turn to dance with me
I have this feeling that you think we're meant to be
Listen to a song that just sounds like you and me

I'm in a dream, baby, you put me to sleep
As you sing a lullaby that would slowly murder me
I'm never right, you should pin the blame on me
Change all our songs to a sad tune melody
I have this fear that one day you'd be bored of me
Throw me aside, bury me under a tree.

Moving On

Where is the devil when you need him the most
When your world is upside down; you're losing hope
Fading faith and falling down not moving on and on
Where is the angel you speak of a lot
When I'm losing all the people I love
Hurting deep, having feelings not moving on and on.

Waiting on Tomorrow

You said you'll do it tomorrow
But tomorrow never comes
And I end up waiting
For you
Forever.

A Moment of Time Where Time Stops

A moment of time where time stops
A memory is written
Feelings are drawn on a fine piece of paper
From all the colors of the light

…

A moment of time where time stops
Everything is the same
20 years later you still can go back
Feelings overwhelm your current state of mind

…

A moment of time where time stops
Surrounded by hope
Captured in the eyes of those we love
As they forever visit us in our dreams

…

A moment of time where time stops
Everyone is happy
And one word would make the dream last
In one voice we all say, "Cheese."

Land of Shame

I lost the will to live when you left me all alone
With the stars all on fire, falling down on my home
We were burning with desire; I had no one else to blame
But the town that I grew up in, known as the land of shame.

My One

I was looking for the one wasting my whole damn life
Not knowing I was looking for one too many
I never realized that it was there all this time
I did not need the one to finally be happy.

After Ache

Ache after ache, we find it hard to breathe
Our legs cannot stand on this solid ground beneath
Once was joyful, now everything seems black
And we are lost in this world, now that we're without a back
Ache after ache, we find it hard to breathe

…

Endless and sleepless nights are now gone
Followed by more endless and sleepless nights
All the pain that once was, is finally undone
And the struggles are over, we no longer have to fight
Ache after ache, we find it hard to breathe

…

But,
We are not alone and together we're strong
We're pure at soul and were survivors all along
We'll manage to smile and be alive again
Since we are used to devastation and constant pain
Ache after ache, we find it hard to breathe.

No Man

I destroy my life with my hands
My heart doesn't want to love this man
This man I am is no man
I am a demon, I'm not human

I'm lost in shame and I'm confused
Caught in this land where I abused
All my rights to stay and I refused
To be happy and live amused

And I lost a lover for a farfetched dream
Who thought my end would be extreme
A beloved friend and a wicked scheme
A doomful fate in a cheerful stream

No one guessed that my life would change
Don't you find it rather strange
Although I try, I cannot arrange
How I feel, I feel estranged.

Cup of Tea

Just another cup of tea
There's no time
You and I
We both are
Made of lies
Now you say
That all you want is one more chance
But I gave you all I could give
Yet you went ahead
And did
What you did
All of this.

Fly Roman Blue

Some dreams require a hollow soul
Some dreams can't be reached at all
Some dreams are bounded to the ground
And some dreams can never be found

…

The happiest color is blue
A color that represents you
All your dreams are colorless
And your life is a big mess

…

Grounded you cannot fly
Now all your dreams are awful lies
Deep in thought you're lost in time
Dreaming has become a crime

…

Only one way to stay true
You have to fly, Roman Blue!

Wilt

It was the smell of your morning coffee that made me wake up every day
Eyes still closed, I walked to you half-asleep following the beautiful pungent scent
Opening my eyes once I am by your side so that your glamorous smile is the first thing I see in the morning
A sunny side up on my plate and a shining sun sparkling in the sky, yet you were the one brightening my day with your stories
I would sit there in my place and listen to them without feeling bored or bothered
I would stand by you as you watered your favorite flower
Now I can no longer stand the smell of coffee as it reminds me of you
Now I open my eyes once I wake up hoping life was a dream
Now I never leave my bed and won't spend a second listening to anyone
Now all my drapes are down as I don't want the sun to shine on my gloomy days
Now your flower is wilted because so has you
Now I no longer exist because you no longer exist, and we no longer are.

Fading Mist

I still find it hard to believe
That anyone can love someone like me
Someone broken yet rude and mean
Someone dying from this pain unseen

…

For deep, deep down, I still believe
That everyone loves me because of fear
They never really care, never held me dear
Kept me around just to have me near

…

I still find it hard to breathe
Around people I'm dying to meet
I miss their smiles and laughs and tears
Yet they only miss the idea of me

…

I ask myself, had I ceased to exist
Will anyone notice, will I be missed
Or would I go away like fading mist
And never have the fate of being reminisced.

Cold Heart

It's raining in July
No clouds in the sky
It's almost midnight
When lighting might strike
On the 15th of July
Now you're all alone
In your room
And it's snowing in August
It's been 13 days since the 6th
And there is someone that you miss
And the leaves fall down
In the saddest day of all
Three days into October
When people start to fall
Nothing ever gets better
For a heart that went so cold
Scorching heat
On the 23rd
Of a joyous, joyful month
The lights go on
Smiles are heard
This is now my favorite month.

Sad Eyes

There is sadness in his eyes
And I can see he hates the lies
He used to claim: immune to cries
There are tears about to fall down
But he isn't gonna frown
He covers them with a thousand smiles
I wanna know what's bothering him
Help him out; comfort him
Wipe his tears away and tell him all will be okay
Let me be here even when no one else
Shows at the door I'll be here to help
He doesn't have to shed a tear
I'll always be here
Yet the sadness in his eyes never fades
It's here to stay
It's his look that's like a blade
I'm hooked; can't go away
It's a waterfall
Of never-ending tears
Yet none of them would seem to fall
They're trapped in there
In his sad eyes
His sad, sad eyes.

I Am Me

I'm not
Who I wanted me to be
And I'm not
Who you wanted me to be
And I'm not
Who my mother prayed day and night for me to be

I am me

And lately I've been saying that it's not bad
I have chased my dreams and I'm glad
That I got to live this life I had
Even though I spent it all being sad

One day I will come to terms with who I am.

Disappear

I am ready to disappear
Go home and hide away…
Hide away my tears
Lock them up with all my fears
Sit in darkness till the light appears
Ready to disappear.

Choice II

I'm choosing to
Give you what you want
The life you always craved
So I'm going away
This way
Things will be okay

…

I'm choosing to
Let you have the girl
Let you live your days
As I just go away
Trust me, This way
Things will be okay

…,

You don't have to choose
I'm doing it for you
I know that we were friends
But all things have to end

…

If you don't know what to do
I'm doing it for you
So you don't have to choose

Guess we were bound to lose
This way
I'm the one who'd lose

No matter what you choose
You can never lose
But I was forced to lose
When I was forced to choose
Me
This way
Someone gets to choose me
Even if it's me.

It Will Always Rain

As a young boy, she was everything he wanted to be
Intelligent, strong, and standing independently
Her hugs were warm as she held him caringly
He loved her the most and her love was motherly

She was this perfect mother, aunt, sister and friend
There was nothing she couldn't fix, no heart she couldn't mend
Around her you could be yourself, no reason to pretend
But just like it always is, all good things come to end

The years went by as she suddenly fell ill and weak
Her perfect smile was fading and she couldn't speak
Memory on and off again, and a poor physique
Chemicals fighting in her brain where havoc was wreaked
He stood by the side and watched her wither away
All of her petals were falling day after day
And all he could do was smile at her and say,
"Don't worry, things are fine, you're going to be okay."

She'd look at him and try to smile through the pain
She'd recognize his face but forget his name
It's not her fault but this tumor to blame
And the look in her eyes is no longer the same

Just like that, one day the wind blew away her flame
She was gone leaving in his heart a stain
He can't help but to tear up at the mention of her name
Now all the days are dark, and it will always rain.

Bow

I will call the devil now
Be prepared to smile and bow
End my life to end the pain
No longer living in vain
Can't manage to be insane
Will not do it all over again.

Devil's Game

There's a riot in my head
All my thoughts make me upset
Everything is black or white
But my mind is grey

There's a battle up ahead
If I lose it, I'd be dead
I have no choice but to fight
There is no other way

If I try to hide instead
My thoughts will leave a trail of bread
It is dark when there is light
No place for me to stay

My thoughts are painting me red
From all the poison that I bled
There is no justice, no wrong, no right
Just the Devil's game to play.

Darkness

When you're tired from all the lies
In the night with the fall of rain
Raise your hands to the skies
You pray it washes all the pain

Stand in the dark soaking wet
Surrounded by your deepest fears
Demons' thoughts that make you upset
Pray the rain would hide your tears

Hope the sound of thunder clouds
Will scatter all your demons scared
Just pray the roar is pretty loud
So they can't hear as you escape

You run away into the night
Hoping things will be okay
You are darkness seeping through the light
Tomorrow is another day.

Mean

I mean
"I'm mean"
But you don't know where I've been
Fighting
Fighting
For the sun to rise again
…
And I've spent 50 days in a cage
And I've spent 80 nights without sleep
And I waste all my days backstage
Just so you have a play to see.
And I never go to see the garden
When I helped planting the seeds
And I feel too much of a burden
Yet I try to fulfill all your needs.

8th Deadly Sin

I'm the devil in sheep's clothing
Even wolves can't outrun me
All the hellhounds fear my footsteps
As they hear me creeping near

I'm a demon with angel wings
With a halo and a harp, I sing
You would think that I'm a blessing
But I'm the 8th deadly sin

I make you think you're crazy
I turn the sane insane
But heed my words
If I come for you
Darling, you will love the pain

I can make you fall in love with me
Everything I say you'd do
If you wonder why, you love me so
It's a spell I cast on you

I'm a charming man with a charming smile
And sweet and dazzling eyes
With a white pure heart, you'd fall for me
And my lovely innocent lies

No matter what I do to you, you will not complain
For I am but a heavenly soul, but you love the pain
Honey, it's not my fault, I'm not to blame
Darling, you love the pain.

Disguise

You call me crazy
But you make me think 'bout you everyday
You make me question my own mindset
…
You made me fall from the skies
I know this house is made of lies
You brought me down, broke my disguise.

Three to One

Born in darkness now back again
Feeling hollow, sadness and pain
Three years back to when the light came
Now it's gone and nothing will be the same
Three years back I had nothing, I was free
I prayed for something, God answered me
I wanted one reason, he gave me three
It used to be I then it changed to we
Now I can't find enough tears to cry
Now I don't have these reasons not to die
Now that the we will become an I
Take away my voice, take away my eye
I don't need to smile or shout anymore
Don't need to talk, don't need to walk
'Cause I can't live like I lived before
All the tears I shed, all the words I spoke
Plant a seed, now the tree is gone
Taken by force, this is law, it is done
Took away my moon, took away my sun
Now I can't hide, I can't lie, I can't run

It is over
I am over
It's getting closer
I'm losing closure
And now the stars are dim
All my thoughts are grim
'Cause my chances were slim.

Sun's Reign

I don't know why I don't believe when people
That even when things are rough, one day they'll be okay
Maybe because all I have ever known is pain
Maybe this is why I hate the sun and love the rain

'Cause when it rains
I can hide away my tears
Forget the pain
And be free from all my fears
And when it's dark
I can cry with silent tears
Forget the past
Stand against my darkest fears

But it never rains
All I've known is constant pain
This is the sun's reign
All I've got is tears and pain.

Empty cage

Every time
I see your empty cage
My heart breaks
Into tiny little pieces
Now the time
Is a bit too late
To celebrate
When the world would free us
And I can't seem to spread my wings and fly
When I know you won't be in the sky
I feel featherless
I don't feel high
Can't escape from this
I don't know why
There is no meaning for a world
Without you by my side
I'm locked up
I'm losing pace
The tide is high
I'm out of place
Nothing will ever be the same
Featherless and
Lost in shame land.

Devil's Game: Wrong

You're quite impressed by agony
You're quite impressed by pain
You say I am your despair
And I am disdain
But you're not quite there
You can think once again
I'm not the kind of devil
That would cause any pain
I take my torture seriously
I'm the poison in your veins
But don't try to rat me out
It would be all in vain
No-one would believe your lies
They'd say you went insane
That's how I do my work
So I'll say it once again
There is no justice, no wrong, no right
It's just the Devil's game.

Kerosene

Kerosene
Burn my skin
Take with you
All my sins
Burn my past
Dear kerosene!
Burn me up
Only then I'll win
Wake me up
When this dream's over
Back to sleep
I will do it over
Let me live it one more time
For with kerosene I will shine!
Like a butterfly flying high
Across the meadows
And through the sky
At night a moth with a darker shell
Took off my wings and then I fell.
Dear kerosene,
Can't you tell?
I'm already burnt
'Cause life is hell.

Sin

So hear me tell you what I did
A story of a sin, a horrible deed
I wish it never came to my head
It can't be undone so listen to me
I was walking down a dark path
And in an alley at midnight
I felt a wave of hatred
I was walking innocently
Never thought I'd hear a shot
Yet every bone in my body
Shivered on the spot
And I couldn't find a way to run away
And I couldn't think of a day there I'll be okay
I wasn't fine! I wasn't safe!
This blood is mine! It became my cape
And I flew
Then I fell… in front of you
You couldn't tell what I could do
To escape that hell
You were too kind; I was too harsh
You did not know what I had in mind
I flew away! Leaving you

Leading them back to you
You thought I did care for you
I thought I did, but then I knew
That
I had to save myself
I had to be alive
I had to let go of you and leave you behind
Another thing that I did wrong
A new mistake; this path is long
And it got darker and the sun won't rise
And the stars are dim. There is no sign of light!
I'm going deeper
Right into the sin
It's getting creeper
Oh, I wish I'd win
To leave this place and leave this path
To go away into eternal wrath
And sleep
Never wake up
And leave
The things I love
I kept walking
I knew it was wrong
I was mistaken, but I didn't mind at all
Yes, I wanted to stop
Yes, I wanted it to end
But I did not and I couldn't
I was asked to tell them what
The sin I did

I'd rather not
I was asked to say the truth
But I couldn't
So I kept walking
Until I fell
Into darkness
My own hell.

I'd rather not
I was asked to say the truth
But I couldn't
So I kept walking
Until I fell
Into darkness
My own hell.

Virtues of Men and Mice

Remorse…
Can't think of anything worse.
Regret…
Any memory to detest.
Guilt!
What makes a flower wilt?
Culpability?
Unlawful liability?
Or a sin?
Something hidden deep within.
A vice…
Virtues of men and mice.
A wicked deed.
Pine over to be freed.
Is any of this real?
Are these the right feelings to feel?
Regret!?
Or is there no reason to fret?

Breaking Bad

I'm breaking bad
You're breaking free
It got you out of my spell
I'm going mad
You're joining me
Insane, we couldn't tell
You were all I had
We were meant to be
And now we're bound to dwell.

Wounds Run Deep

There's a demon in my head
Who shouts, "JUST LET THINGS END!"
There's a monster under my bed
Who I wish would kill me dead

And I try to sleep
To forget this pain I feel
But it runs too deep
These wounds won't seem to heal

Every single word that was said
Breaks a heart that I can never mend
And the demon smiles and writes in my head,
"Just give up, you have no true friend."

I try to shout and I try to scream
But no one wants to hear how I truly feel
And I say to myself this has to be a dream
But this pain in my heart is just too real

I'm finally choosing myself
I've been by my side like nobody else

Through thick and thin
Through right and wrong
And for every sin
I would sing a song

And I know that I've been broken before
But I can't take heartbreak anymore

And I know that you don't seem to care
You think that a guy like me can be found anywhere
So I'm closing my eyes, I'll be headed somewhere
Where the pain would disappear and the skies are fair.

Tall

It's dark and raining; I'm outside
This aching pain that's deep inside
I mourn the loss
I never thought I'd mourn
Now I'm tired and I'm worn

…

Your room is empty; I am scared
I'm filled with agony and despair
And all the songs I ever wrote
Started with your name
Now they'll never be the same

…

I fell from love
And fell from pain
I stood before
So I'll stand again
I never stayed down on the floor
So I stand tall

…

I fell in love
I fell for you
I was all in

I knew it's true
I don't have you by my side
And I miss you
And I need you
…
But I stand so tall
And I would not fall.

A Wrong to Fix a Wrong

It's like you have to wait until
All the pain is gone
Took a simple pill
Played a different song
Something new but still
You tried to sing along
Then took another pill
A wrong to fix a wrong

It's such a big deal
But you claim it's not
Your thoughts are surreal
Now you sleep a lot
Skipping every meal
To curl up in your spot
Forgetting how to feel
"Cheers," another shot

Lost in your mind
Starting to give up
To leave it all behind
You fill another cup

Life was not kind
It set this whole thing up
To think that you were blind
You're about to blow up

So you do it all again
To forget the pain
Looping that one song,
"A wrong to fix a wrong."

New Obsession

It's a feeling of oppression
But they claim, "You're not oppressed."
It's a feeling of depression
But you say, "I'm not depressed."
It's the way you feel at night
When your darkness eats the lights
And there's nothing you could say
That would make you feel okay
So you try to close your eyes
Just to reach the next day
…
And when the lights are out,
All your demons start to shout
And your mind is wide awake
And your heart is full of ache
Your worst nightmares start to scream
Feeding off all your dreams
ALL the good things that you've seen
They all now seem unseen

As your demons scream:
"WAKE UP! DON'T SLEEP! This is hell, it's not a dream!"
"STAY AWAKE! YOU FREAK! You will break 'cause you
are weak!"

…

It's a feeling of oppression
And you know you are oppressed
It's a feeling of depression
God knows you are depressed
It's a feeling of repression
Tears became a new obsession
As you try to shut away
All your demons everyday
But things will never go your way
And you'll never be okay

…

So you try to close your eyes
Just to reach the next day.

Devil's Game: Right

When you need me, I'll be by your side
To make sure you're feeling okay

I will charm you under my command
When I sing to you, you will sway

Then you'll feel happy and happier
You'll be begging me to stay

'Cause you know how much I care
Even when I'm far, far away

And when you're feeling down and broken
I will try my best to brighten your day

But there isn't much I can do
When things start to go the other way

For there is no justice, no wrong, no right
Just the Devil's game to play.

Little Piece of Bread

There's that little piece of bread
That I eat late night in bed
Just a little something to feed the demons in my head

There's this sad song that I write
About justice, wrong, and right
Just to soothe my demons, so they don't start a fight

There are some scars on my skin
Reminding me of all my sins
Battle wounds from the fights I fought within

There's this demon inside of me
Consuming my whole body
Little by little destroying me

No-one hears my silent screams
No-one sees my late-night tears
No-one knows my deepest fears

There's this piece of bread I eat
In my bed so my demons feed
On that bread instead of me
A little piece of bread instead of me.

The Demons' Song

Wide awake, turning in bed
As the night begins to creep
Demons crawling in my head
They won't let me go to sleep
Letting out their loudest cries
As I try to count the sheep
And among their thousand lies
There's a truth hiding deep
Then it starts to get to me
And my heart begins to weep
As they all sing in euphony,
"What you sow is what you reap."

The Ghost from Your Stories

I'm the ghost from your stories
A king from the past
I am fame and glory
But good things never last
May this be memento mori
I am sorry

It's darker nowadays and my heart is empty
I've mended all my ways but my past is hefty
Wounded on the floor since the day that you left me
For you envy

Dreaming of a sky that is nothing but blue
Reminiscing on the times that I spent here being true
Painting pictures on our walls telling stories of me and you
Now I am rubber and you are glue

They say slowly all good things come to end
Sometimes it's too fast, there's no time to comprehend
Picking up pieces of the lies in a heart you can never mend
Visions of a shadow of a friend

I will rise to the skies nothing can keep me down forever
Forget the good old happy days that you and I spent together
When we said we'll never be apart I guess now is never
I don't care whatsoever

I might be the ghost from all your stories
But I'm the king in mine
Rising from the ashes of my past glory
You should know I'll be fine
You don't even have to worry
Trust me when I say, you'll be the one who is sorry.

Break into Whole

I feel broken
Chosen to
I feel hated
Trusted to
To repair your heart
To mend every soul I see
To reflect my love onto every single person that needs
But I won't give up although I'm broken
I won't let go because I was chosen to be the one
To help the world
And I won't give up
Because they need me
Or that is what I tell myself every night
Yet I won't give up
I save every love except mine
It's lost for good
And I help everyone except me
Because it's no good
I won't give up
Although I'm dying
And I won't let go
I'll keep on trying

To make the world a better place
To break my heart into a thousand pieces
And give every person one
So, I can live on forever.

Messed Up

I'd rather write than open up
I know it's right to bottle up
All my emotions and the feelings I'm feeling
I'd rather hide away my fears
I'd rather drown myself in tears
Than show people the feelings that I feel
…
Even if I wanted to talk I can't
It's like my tongue was eaten by a cat
Every time I try to speak I can't
The words escape my mind and soul
…
Even when I try to open up
Even when my lies are piling up
I even realize I'm messing up
I'm messing up
I'm messed up and messing up
But I can't seem to help myself at all
…
I cannot tell you what's wrong
I never can let you in
Because everyone

I ever let in
Is either gone
Or on their way away
And I'm always alone
By the end of the day.

Devil's Game: Justice

This is a sad world we live in
There's no-one you can trust or believe
Everyone has a deadly sin
Inner demons they have to feed

And the deepest wounds you'll get
Is from your dearest friends
You either live with regret
Or spend your life planning revenge

It is Justice that you seek
So you can finally fall asleep
But there is no such thing as Justice
There are golden words please trust this

'Tis a sad world we live in
People divide to choose sides
Everyone driven by their pride
They're all pointing a finger to blame

’Tis a sad world we live in

Everyone fights for their rights

But there’s no justice, no wrong, no right

It’s just the Devil’s game… that we play… such pity, such shame.

Nothing Left to Do

Lack of sleep
Or a slumber deep
You will always wake up with an ache in your heart
Head that hurts
Or about to burst
You can never make it go away once it starts
Out of air
You're feeling scared
This is just another normal day for you
Your hands will shake
Heart begins to ache
'Cause you know there's nothing left for you to do.

Memories

This feeling is like striking thunder
Burning my heart in its slumber
Weakening me and breaking my might
Keeping me up alone in the night
Staring blindly right through the dark
Got nothing on my mind but this ominous mark
…
And it burns so badly
This scar on my back and my forehead
And I'm losing track and I'm misled
Is this all in my head?
All my memories are burning up in flames
I'm caught up in the price I had to pay for fame
All my memories are burning up in flames
And I'm tired of playing those childish games
And I die to the thought that nothing's the same.

My Only Clock Is Broken

Time doesn't seem to be moving
Every day is the very same day

…

It's a constant loop of pain
The same agony again and again
Every day I do not feel okay

…

Stuck in time and space
Waiting till I can leave this place
Every day I wait for that day

…

Now my heart is broken
And all the clocks have spoken,
"Time is not moving on ever again."

9:00

Nine strikes the clock
Running out of air
Gasping for freedom
Trapped in nowhere
Eyes wide open
Dreams kept shut
Searching for people
In this empty hut

Nine strikes the clock
Tears that don't fall down
Left to decay
In this desolate town
Heart now broken
Praying for a mend
Fallen in a pit
Searching for a friend

Nine strikes the clock
Now lost in time
Stuck in the moment
The clock would still strike nine.

When Worlds Collide

When worlds collide
Someone's bound to get hurt
We divide
Can't have the best of both worlds
You have to choose
Or you will also lose

When worlds collide
Balance is shifted
You're not blind
You can see all that they did
You have to choose
Or you will also lose

When worlds collide.

Heartbreak

Now I'm all alone
In an empty room
With a lonely rose
That can never bloom.

More Than Ever

I love you now
Like I loved you then
Except
I love you now
More than ever
And I will keep loving you
No matter what happens between us
No matter where you go
I will keep loving you
Even when you leave
Even when I'm all alone in a crowded room
I will feel your presence
Reassuring my soul
And comforting me
And I will love you at that moment
Like I loved you when we first met
Like I loved you with all my heart
Even when we became apart.

By My Side

I wish you were always by my side
Sometimes the good memories are not enough

Without having you by my side
Life has been tougher than tough

And all the lies that I lied
To try to smoothen what is rough

Have only hurt me and my pride
Deep down I shout enough is enough

And all the methods that I tried
Have been called out as a bluff

And all the nights that I cried
Would've been easier with your love

Deep Breath

And the memories that we hide
Deep within us everyday

Like the last time that you smiled
Three seconds before you went away

Will always be in our hearts and minds
Keeping us sane, when we're not okay

And we're not okay.

Lost Another

You lost a brother
Who was forever
By your side when you were alone
You lost another
A potential lover
Who loved you like no one can do
And now you stand on a bottomless floor
The world is gone mad; you're losing control
And now you sail through a thunderstorm
The tide is high, you are losing control

If you ever thought that you'd survive
You won't be here by my side.

Blue Bird

They say there's a bird that is flying up to heaven!
With feathers blue as the sky
With wings made of clouds
That bird leaves the ground
And finds her way up to heaven

…

From a cage to a zoo
She was broken just like you
Always was outspoken
All the time!
She had a voice that used to cure
All the hearts that were so pure
By making them feel loved and alive

…

And now it's time for the sun to set
Don't shed a tear, don't be upset
That little blue bird is making her way through the sky
To the heavens so high

…

My little blue bird
You left without saying goodbye
And no-one ever knew why

Why a bird like you
Would do the things you used to do
You left without saying goodbye

…

Tomorrow the sun won't rise again
Tomorrow it will start to rain
The moment we won't feel the pain
Is the moment we will meet again.

Somewhere Where
the Skies Are Fair

There's a demon in my head
Who shouts, "JUST LET THINGS END!"
There's a monster under my bed
Who wishes I would kill me dead

And when I go to sleep
To forget this pain I feel
Wounds that run too deep
And they won't seem to heal

Every single word that was said
To a broken heart that now mends
And the demon smiles and writes in my head,
"Don't even try, this is where it ends."

I try to shout and I try to scream
But no one wants to hear how I truly feel
And I say to myself I will follow my dream
And this pain in my heart is just not real

I'm finally choosing myself
I've been by my side like nobody else

Through thick and thin
Through right and wrong
Forgive every sin
Always sing along

And I know that I've been broken before
And I faced many heartbreaks so what's one more

And I know that they don't seem to care
They think that a heart like mine can be found anywhere
So I'm moving on, I'll be headed somewhere
where the pain would disappear, and the skies are fair.

Broken Dreams

It's like you walk barefoot on broken glass
Wanting to go back to the perfect past
But time keeps moving us apart
Though you are alone in my heart
I used to smile but not anymore
You are mine and that's for sure
All I want is a glimpse of your pretty face
Take me back to the past to those happy days
Where we used to hang out
No interruptions no guilt
Yet now they intrude
They force themselves and that's rude
Don't they know there is no room
In my heart for it holds one and that's you
Let me know if this is mutual
It's not just me your love is punctual
I want to be where you will always be
And I'll run a thousand miles for thee
All you have to do is look at me.

The Devil Will Never Retire

First the world fell apart
When you fell from my heart
Then the world came to end
When my heart wouldn't mend
All I needed was to lie in bed and rest
Tried to help myself get up and get dressed
Watch my world burn as I fall asleep
Blame it all on you
Because you cut me too deep
Let's watch the world burn
Light up the sky
Watch the devil return
Along your lie
Set it all on fire
'Cause the devil will never retire
Now the world is almost gone
'Cause we are almost done
And tomorrow, no more world
For the heart you wouldn't hold
Watch the world burn up in flames
Baby it's your fault; know you're to blame.

Find Myself

Tried to find myself
'Cause I couldn't see me in the mirror
Couldn't find me in the phonebook
Nor my secret, secret journal
My name wasn't in any entry
In my 20 diaries
So, I got up the courage to start my enquiries
Now I ask the ones who claim to be my friends
Do they know me?
And I ask a question that I know I will regret
Do you know me?
I am a nobody, in an empty world, filled with 'somebodies'
I know I don't exist, for when I die, I won't be missed
And I don't matter in my eyes like the ones that matter in your
eyes
I can read through your lies
Although I am crying, my reflection smiles
I've been living this lie for a while
Been wearing this stupid mask
To stop questions from being asked,
"How come this?" "Who caused that?" "Why is there a scar
on your back?"

"What is this?" "Where is that?" So many questions and the answers I lack…
Or maybe I only have one
I don't know
For I don't know me.

Butterfly

I once stepped on a butterfly
I hoped she didn't die
But that's not how things work in real life.

Destiny

Nobody chose their date of birth
Their name, their height, and place on Earth
'Cause such things; out of our control
We choose them not; oh, not at all
…
Some days we try to fix mistakes
For a broken heart that always aches
But we fail 'cause it's destiny
It is our fate, it's meant to be.

My Heart Spoke During Dinner

My father said we have to talk
The food is cold, the night is long
I felt the water boil as he spoke

My mother knew I will ignite
the convo then I'll start a fight
Although he's wrong, he thinks that he's right.

Dear God, I know I don't believe
I have no faith inside of me
I lost it all when I was fourteen

I was too young to feel the pain
Now agony has struck again
My father told me that I'm insane

He looked at me with all his pride
and told me that my heart has lied
and I should throw my feelings aside

I stood so fast; I was confused
I told him that this is abuse
My mother told me I was being rude

I told her what I knew I can
I still am your little man
That you taught should trust his feelings

This is absurd; it's who I am
I'm more than just a piece of ham
I too have a heart that is beating

I have a soul, this should convey
My feelings are here to stay
I'm not ashamed to say that I am

Gaining nothing from what you say
I am convinced that it's okay
to be proud to say that I am.

Demon Thoughts

This is just a lie
You're being played

No-one really loves you
All the hearts are filled with hate

You don't deserve to have this
Nothing you did was this great

Because you broke many hearts
So you really should be scared

Now you reap what you sow
And you'll live by what you create.

Despair, Agony, and Distress

When I'm all alone, I can see myself
Staring through the mirror at someone else
Fading smiles and a fading gleam
Lost in thoughts of fading dreams

Under my skin, I burn in flames
With no-one else but me to blame
Ice cold water doesn't ease the pain
Of this fire moving in my veins

All they ever do is stand there
And they gawk and gossip and stare
How can I ever feel your heart
If you choose to keep us apart

I'm guilty of all this mess;
Despair, agony, and distress
Am I only me when I'm in pain
A bathroom floor with a bloody stain

When I'm by myself, I can see the truth
I'm stripping myself of my inner youth
On the inside I'm just a fragile flower
Constantly crying every time I shower

But all my tears won't heal my wounds
And my heart will never bloom
Just let me be, go live your lives
And use my soul as a way to survive.

My Heart Spoke
During Dinner – Reflection

We talked tonight
Never really spoke
Since our last fight
Didn't wanna talk
But it's alright
I gave them another chance to
Speak their mind
But they never really wanted
To hear me out
My heart felt erupted
But I couldn't shout
…
They're in my head
Everything they say
Makes me upset
And I'm not okay
I do regret
That I chose to stay
I should've fled
But it doesn't really matter
I gave it all I've got

Though my pride did shatter
It wasn't all for naught
…
My heart spoke during dinner
And God, I know I'm not a sinner
This is a fight without a winner
Where we all will fall down
…
I don't know if it was the right thing to do
Boy, I should have listened to you
They're not ready to face the truth
Yet…

Red

I only see red
Such a dread
I am screaming in my head

I am fading light
I'm losing sight
And the world is black and white

I only see red
Such a dread
Flowing lovely right ahead

I am going mad
I'm feeling sad
And the world is rotting bad

I only see red
Such a dread
And a body is lying dead

I go ahead to see
This can't be
That body belongs to me.

Fading

Fading slowly
Losing my smile
Colors washing away
Darker than black
I disappear.

Freedom

What can break a broken heart?
What can pull two worlds apart?
Drag your soul right to the dark
And send you flying back to the start?

What can fade your smiles to frowns
Turn your worlds all upside down
Suffocate the air all around
Grasping for freedom as you start to drown

What can become all that you miss
Build up a hell from what once was a bliss
Deep in your slumber, you can't escape this
For there's no such thing as true love's kiss

What can erase what was there for many years
Where all you had to do was open up your ears
Now you have to stand and wipe all your tears
Fight all your demons and face all your fears

You know within that it's the right thing to do
Don't wait for dark skies to suddenly turn blue
Heed my words, God knows they are true
You're the only one who's always there for you.

Untitled for Now

A new journey is about to begin
I think I found myself deep within
This is who I want to be
I have to start this new journey

The path I took was not for me
It's not what I want; it's not meant to be
I'm fed up of wearing this huge pretend
I cannot start from where it ends

This has to be a brand-new start
This is gonna be what mends my heart
But I don't know when, and I can't see how
So I'll remain untitled for now.